21st Century Skills Library

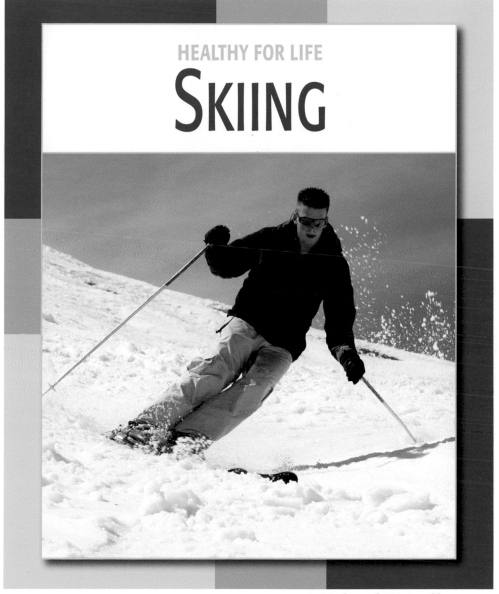

HEALTHY FOR LIFE

SKIING

Michael Teitelbaum

Cherry Lake Publishing
Ann Arbor, Michigan

Published in the United States of America by Cherry Lake Publishing
Ann Arbor, MI
www.cherrylakepublishing.com

Content Adviser: Thomas Sawyer, EdD, Professor of Recreation and Sports Management,
Indiana State University, Terre Haute, Indiana

Photo Credits: Pages 5, 6, 13, and 17, Photo courtesy of Scott A. Smith; page 23,
© Dimitri Iundt/TempSport/Corbis

Library of Congress Cataloging-in-Publication Data
Teitelbaum, Michael.
  Skiing : by Michael Teitelbaum.
    p. cm. — (Healthy for life)
  Includes index.
  ISBN-13: 978-1-60279-015-5 (lib.bdg.)   978-1-60279-091-9 (pbk.)
  ISBN-10: 1-60279-015-9 (lib.bdg.)   1-60279-091-4 (pbk.)
  1. Skis and skiing—Juvenile literature. I. Title. II. Series.
  GV854.315.T45 2008
  796.93—dc22   2007003892

*Cherry Lake Publishing would like to acknowledge the work of
The Partnership for 21st Century Skills.
Please visit* www.21stcenturyskills.org *for more information.*

TABLE OF CONTENTS

CHAPTER ONE

WHOOSH!

*Young or old, anyone can ski! All it takes is a few lessons,
the right equipment, and some common sense.*

You are gliding effortlessly down the mountain, watching the whole world pass by you. You feel as if you're flying, moving as fast as you'll ever move without using a motor. Welcome to the world of skiing!

The good news for you is that, unlike some sports, anyone can ski. It takes no specialized talents or particular physical build—just a few lessons, practice, and common sense. Kids as young as four and folks into their eighties and nineties can do it. This means that if you start skiing now, it's something you can do for the rest of your life.

Basically, skiing is allowing gravity to pull you down a snow-covered mountain while standing on two long, thin boards. Skis come in many shapes and sizes, but they all do basically the same thing—help you zoom down a snowy ski run.

Skiers the world over, at all levels of experience, enjoy their sport at ski resorts. These destinations provide skis and other equipment that you can

Ski resorts can be found in many cold, snowy places around the world.

rent, a lodge to relax in with a hot chocolate after skiing or during a break, a ski lift to carry you up to the top of the mountain, and—most important of all—the mountain and the snow!

Every ski mountain at a resort is divided into different trails, starting from the easier trails for beginners to the most difficult ones for the very

Ski lifts carry skiers and snowboarders to the top of a snowy mountain.

experienced skiers. You'll advance only at a pace that you are comfortable with, so you always feel safe and in control.

One thing you won't be able to control is the condition of the snow or the weather. The best skiing is done on fresh powder that has been smoothed down. The worst condition is icy slopes. Ski resorts do their best to groom the slopes, but the weather can affect ski conditions day-to-day and even hour-to-hour.

As with many sports, overcoming your fear is half the battle. And the best way to do that is by always using the right equipment and by getting the proper training. Before you know it, you'll be whooshing down the slopes!

21st Century Content

Skiing is especially popular in mountainous regions. Ski resorts line the slopes of the Italian, Swiss, and Austrian Alps and the Rocky Mountains. Because of new technology, skiing has also become popular in regions without much snow. Snow-making machines allow people in warmer places like Shanghai, China, to enjoy skiing, too. Shanghai has Asia's largest indoor ski park.

Here are some Web sites that list ski resorts in the United States and around the world:

- www.goski.com/ — Click on "US resorts" or "Global resorts," and you're on your way!
- www.skiresorts.com/ — Select a place to ski by resort or by region.

CHAPTER TWO

WHAT YOU NEED: EQUIPMENT AND TRAINING

Having good equipment that fits correctly is a key to becoming a successful skier. But ski equipment can be very expensive. Also, the boots that fit you this winter may be too small when next ski season rolls around. What to do? In a word: rent!

All ski resorts have a rental shop where they can help you find the right equipment to make skiing a fun and safe experience. Let's take a look at what you'll need.

You can't just wear regular shoes or boots to go skiing. You need

Having the right equipment is essential to enjoying the sport, and wearing proper ski boots are no exception to this rule.

special ski boots. Ski boots are made up of several parts. The outside is a hard plastic shell. On this shell are a series of buckles that snap shut to hold the boot on your feet.

Inside the hard shell is the liner. This soft piece of foam molds to the shape of your foot and also helps keep your feet warm out on the slopes. Your ski boots should fit the way your sneakers do, with a little bit of room in the front so you can wiggle your toes.

In addition to keeping your feet warm, your ski boots also support your feet against the pressure that builds up as you make your way down the hill. They are shaped to set your feet in the perfect position for skiing. They also let you bend your ankles to help keep your balance. Most important, they send energy from your feet and legs to your skis, which allow you to control the direction in which you ski, kind of like a steering wheel in a car.

Getting boots that fit is a very important part of enjoying your skiing experience. Make sure they're not too small. While you may need to twist your foot a little to get it in the boot, if it feels like you're cramming it in, you may need a larger size. If you lean forward in the boot once they are buckled and your heel lifts up while the rest of your foot stays down, the boots are too big. If walking around in the boots for a minute or two makes your foot hurt, the boots are too small. Even though you are anxious to get out onto the slopes, take that extra few minutes to make sure you choose the right size boot. It will mean the difference between a great day of skiing and a horrible one.

Bindings are a piece of equipment that attach to the top of your skis and connect your skis to your boots. They also help to cut down the chance of injury if you fall. During some falls, your skis can send a lot of force to your legs, causing injuries. If too much force comes from your skis into your bindings, the bindings will release the skis from the boots before this force reaches your legs.

Your skis are what get you through the snow and down the mountains. The front end of your ski is called the tip. The tip is curved upward so it can go up and over chunks of snow instead of digging down into them and slowing you down or making you fall. The bottom, or base, of your skis is made of a smooth plastic that is very slippery, to help you glide through the snow, but tough enough to take a beating on run after run down the mountain. The sides of your skis, called edges, are metal strips that help the skis stay straight and keep you from slipping sideways.

Very young children don't need poles. So if you started skiing when you were four or five, you probably didn't use them. But older beginners (like kids your age) need poles, and as you progress to more difficult trails, poles can be a valuable addition to your ski equipment. They help

Poles help skiers stay in control.

you keep your balance and control your downhill ride when going fast or making lots of turns.

The main part of the pole is called the shaft and is usually made of aluminum tubing. The part you hold in your hands is called the grip. Grips have straps attached to them so you don't lose your poles as you zoom along. The round disc at the pointy end of the pole is called the basket. It stops your pole from sinking into deep, soft snow.

To pick the right size pole, use this trick. Stand up straight and hold the pole upside down, with your elbow bent, grasping it just below the basket. Place the grip onto the ground just in front of you. Is your forearm parallel to the ground? Then your pole is the perfect size. If your forearm is lower than parallel, the pole is too short. If it's higher than parallel, the pole is too long.

Although ski helmets used to be just for downhill racers and very little kids (under age six), more and more skiers are wearing helmets these days. They are lightweight, help keep heat from leaving your body, and are added protection against head injuries. Simply put, it's a good idea to wear a helmet while skiing.

The trick to having fun and successful days on the slopes is to dress so you don't get too cold or too hot. The best way to do this is by dressing in layers—three layers, to be exact. The first layer you put on is called the base layer. This is usually long underwear made of a special polyester fabric. The problem with wearing a cotton base layer is that when you start sweating, it gets wet—and stays wet. Now you've got wet clothes up against your skin, which makes you uncomfortable and cold. The great thing about the polyester fabric is that it removes the wetness through a process called wicking. Wicking moves the wetness away from your skin to the outside of the fabric, where it evaporates.

The second layer is the insulation layer. A shirt, jacket, or vest made of fleece (also a polyester fabric) is a perfect insulation layer. Its purpose is to provide warmth. The third layer is the shell layer. This goes on top of everything else and protects you from wind, snow, or rain. A nylon jacket is a perfect shell layer.

To enjoy your skiing experience, wear clothing that keeps you loose, comfortable, warm, and dry.

Learning & Innovation Skills

Renting ski equipment is a must for beginners. Once you know you love the sport and will be doing it often, you can begin saving up for your own stuff. Depending on the location, you can rent your ski equipment for between $15 and $30 per day. Here's what it costs to buy your gear:

1) Boots: $50–$300
2) Bindings: $70–$200
3) Poles: $25–$75
4) Skis: $60–$300
5) Helmets: $30–$100

Which piece of equipment would you save up for first? Why?

Just as they are important anytime you go out to play in the snow—even if it's just to build a snowman or have a snowball fight—gloves and a hat keep you warm while skiing. Tinted goggles are also a huge help. The tint acts like sunglasses to keep out the glare from the bright white slopes, and the strapped-on goggles keep the wind and snow out of your eyes.

In skiing, training and fitness go hand in hand. However, the most important thing you can do to prepare to ski is to take a lesson. No one is born knowing how to ski. And it's not something you pick up in gym class, or in the schoolyard, or just playing with your friends. Get lessons at the ski resort before you ski for the first time. This will set a foundation for all the skiing you do for the rest of your life.

CHAPTER THREE

STAYING SAFE ON THE SLOPES

The ski patrol transports an injured skier off the slopes.

Everybody's seen pictures of skiers being carried off the slopes. The image of a skier sitting in the lodge, leg in a cast, sipping hot chocolate, and wishing he or she could be back out on the slopes, is as common as the image of a skier actually skiing.

With every new sport you learn, you will learn new *etiquette*. *Etiquette* is a set of rules for proper behavior in a certain situation. For example, eating etiquette includes using a napkin, not talking with your mouth full, and waiting to eat until everyone is served.

Skiing etiquette is important not only to be polite but also to be safe. Here are some tips:

1) Only ski trails that are right for your skill level. Trails are marked as beginner, intermediate, difficult, and expert.

2) Use the ski lift properly. If you don't know how, watch others first. Don't be afraid to ask the lift operator for help.

3) Always be aware of the skiers in front of you. It's your responsibility to stay out of their way.

But that injured skier doesn't have to be you, if you use the right equipment and some common sense. Wearing the right boots and bindings (ones that fit properly) greatly reduce the chance of injuries.

First, be sure to take a lesson before hitting the slopes. The basic techniques you'll learn will help keep you injury free. Never attempt to ski a more advanced slope than you are ready for. Make sure you are in control of your speed at all times. Never go so fast that you feel out of control.

Stay focused even if you are skiing beginner trails. Don't daydream. You can take in the beautiful scenery, but keep your mind on what you are doing. Also, never ski if you feel tired. Sit down for a while, relax, have a snack, and get your energy back before returning to the slopes. Keep clear of trees, the lift, the outside edges of the trail, and, of course, other skiers!

*To avoid injury, be sure to take a ski lesson
or two before hitting the slopes.*

Never jump while skiing unless you know you have a safe, smooth place to land. If you do jump, always land on both skis at the same time and keep your knees bent.

If you fall, keep your knees bent and don't try to stop the fall with your arms. Also, don't try to get up until you've stopped sliding. Most falls result in no injury, so stay calm and wait until you glide to a stop. Then get up slowly.

Falls aren't the only danger in skiing. In addition to all the equipment and clothing discussed in chapter two, one of the most important pieces of skiing safety equipment is sunscreen. That's right, sunscreen! Just because it isn't summer and you're not at the beach, lake, or pool doesn't mean that you can't get badly sunburned. High up on a mountain, surrounded by

When proper precautions are neglected, skiing can lead to serious injury.

white snow that reflects the sun's harmful rays, you can do quite a bit of damage to your skin. Always use a sunscreen with an SPF of at least 30.

Also, beware of frostbite. A long day out in the cold can seriously damage your skin, or worse. Cover up as much skin as possible—hands, face, neck, etc. If any part of your skin starts to feel numb or overly cold, get inside. Usually just being in a warm building will do the trick, but if your fingers just won't warm up, place them in warm—NOT HOT!—water. They have to warm up slowly, and hot water could damage the skin further.

The most serious cold-weather problem you can face is hypothermia. This is an extreme drop in your body's temperature. Very cold temperatures can cause hypothermia, but so can being wet and being out in cold weather (even if it's above freezing). Hypothermia is a potentially life-threatening condition, but its early symptoms are easy to spot. If you're out in the cold and your teeth start chattering or you start shivering, get inside quickly and warm

21st Century Content

Skiing is a great *cardiovascular* activity. *Cardio* is the Latin word for "heart." Vascular refers to the blood vessels which carry oxygen to your body.

Cardiovascular exercise helps you stay active longer, without running out of breath. These cardiovascular activities will keep you in shape when you're off the slopes:

- Walking
- Jogging
- Swimming
- Bicycling
- Inline Skating
- Rowing
- Cross-country skiing

up. These are the early signs of hypothermia and you have plenty of time to take action before things get more serious. The best way to prevent hypothermia is to dress warmly (don't forget those layers), take breaks to warm up, and stay dry.

If you are skiing in higher altitudes (elevations over 8,000 feet (2,500 meters) in places like the Rocky Mountains, you could experience altitude sickness. The air at those altitudes has less oxygen, so you might feel dizzy, out of breath, and have a terrible headache. The best way to prevent altitude sickness is to give your body time to adjust to the thinner air. Relax for your first day or two before going to the slopes, and then go at it slowly, taking frequent breaks. Also, drink lots and lots of water to keep from getting dehydrated.

CHAPTER FOUR

BEING A GOOD GUEST: SKIING RESPONSIBLY

*Part of the fun of skiing is enjoying the outdoors
and taking in the breathtaking scenery.*

As with all outdoor sports, half the fun of skiing is being in the great

big beautiful outdoors. Enjoying the beauty of nature in the winter goes

hand in hand with the thrill of zipping down a mountain. And so, the

same classic rule that is true for camping, hiking, picnicking, or visiting

Skiers take responsibility for each other. Even if a skier heads down the slope alone, he or she may need others for help.

What do you do if you're gliding down the mountain and you come upon an injured skier?

- Take off your skis and stand them up in the snow, above the injured person, in the shape of an X to warn other skiers that someone is hurt.

- Talk to the injured skier. Is he or she unconscious, dizzy, bleeding? Find out as much as you can about the person's condition.

- Wave down another skier and ask that person to go to the nearest lift, where the operator can radio the ski patrol to come to the aid of the injured person.

- Never try to move the injured person. Wait with him or her until the ski patrol arrives.

a park also applies to skiing: *if you carry it in, carry it out!* In other words, don't leave any trash behind. Wrappers from snacks and empty water bottles should be placed into trash cans.

Your main responsibility on a ski slope is to the other skiers. Just like a good driver has to follow the traffic rules, a responsible skier has a set of rules that must be followed.

You must remain in control. That means, don't go too fast, don't go on trails that you're not ready for, and always stay aware of the skiers around you.

Remember, the skiers in front of you have the right-of-way. It's your job to avoid colliding with them by slowing down if you're getting too close. After all, you can see them, but—unless they have eyes in the back of their heads—they can't see you.

Don't stop suddenly (unless it's an emergency) or block the trail for the people coming down the hill behind you. You'll have

Alberto Tomba won the gold medal in the giant slalom event at both the 1998 and the 1992 Olympics.

plenty of time to call your friend on the cell phone when you reach the bottom of the run.

If the trail you are on connects to another trail, slow down and check to see if anyone is coming down before you turn onto the new trail.

Obey warning signs on the slopes. Your safety depends on it.

Always obey posted signs and warnings. If a trail is closed, it's for a good reason, most likely due to a dangerous situation.

Common sense can go a long way toward a fun and safe ski experience. Be courteous and look out for other skiers—you'll have a great time, and so will everyone else!

CHAPTER FIVE

THE ADDED BONUS:
HEALTH BENEFITS OF SKIING

In skiing, training and fitness go hand in hand. As mentioned earlier, to learn the techniques of skiing, you must take a lesson. But since in most places, the ski season lasts for just a few months—and you'll probably

Skiing is great exercise for the whole family!

only get to go skiing a couple of times a season—you need to train year-round. That's right, you must train off the slopes. Skiers call this dryland training.

Training in the off-season helps you build up the endurance you need to ski longer and better.

Aerobic training such as walking, running, or cycling helps you build up the endurance you need to ski longer and better. It also has the health benefit of relieving stress, helping you lose weight, and making your heart healthier.

Strength training builds up muscles, and strong muscles help you ski more easily. Be sure to work your upper body muscles, stomach muscles, and leg muscles. The added benefit of strength training is that there is no better way to prevent injuries than by building up your muscles.

As with any sport, stretching once your muscles are warmed up is helpful. It increases your flexibility and circulation, allowing you to move more easily. And stretching loosens up the muscles, making it

21st Century Content

Compare the approximate number of calories a 100-pound (45-kilogram) person burns in one hour of skiing to the number burned in one hour of these other activities. If you weigh less, you'll burn fewer calories in the same amount of time. If you weigh more, you'll burn more calories in the same amount of time:

Skiing (downhill): 396
Cross-country skiing: 472
Rock climbing: 198
Playing basketball: 498
Running: 456
Backpacking: 318
Swimming: 276
Bowling: 138
Playing Frisbee: 138
Brushing your teeth: 114
Talking on the phone: 48
Watching TV or playing video games: 48

Most people ski just for the fun of it, without ever thinking about how fast they're moving down the mountain. But those dreaming of Olympic gold become ski racers, trying to beat the clock. Here are some of the ski races you'll see every four years at the Olympics:

- Slalom—In this race, skiers must pass through a series of gates spaced close together, making one sharp turn after another.
- Giant Slalom—This is a version of slalom in which the gates are farther apart and the skiers make bigger, slower turns.
- Super-G—Although this event does include some gates like those in giant slalom races, it mostly involves following a twisting path down the mountain.
- Downhill—The name says it all. It's straight down the hill at speeds of more than 70 miles (115 kilometers) per hour in the premiere skiing event of the Olympics.

less likely you'll strain or pull them. Your off-season stretching routine will be a huge benefit once you get back on the slopes.

There are a few other sports that help train you for skiing in the off-season. Many of the leg movements and the techniques used to achieve balance for in-line skating are the same as those used for skiing. Mountain biking helps you learn how to come down a mountain while looking ahead, planning your route from point to point in order to avoid dangerous obstacles. That's exactly what you do while skiing, too.

Keep fit, learn and practice the skills, train, warm up, cool down, stretch, and get the right equipment—and soon you'll be flying without wings down a snowy slope!

You do not need mountains to enjoy skiing. Cross-country skiing is also great fun.

GLOSSARY

bindings (BINE-dingz) the equipment that attaches the ski to the boot

dryland training (DRY-land TRANE-ingh) exercises for preparation for skiing off the slopes, not on snow

etiquette (E-ti-kut) rules of behavior

frostbite (FROHST-bite) a condition in which skin freezes after being in the cold too long

groom (GRUME) to care for the ski slopes by using machines that keep it smooth and safe for skiing

lift (LIHFT) a device that carries skiers up to the top of the mountain

lodge (LAHDGE) a building at a ski resort where skiers can rest and get food

powder (POW-duhr) soft, fluffy snow

resorts (rih-ZORTS) places where people go to ski

slopes (SLOWPS) the parts of the mountain with the trails that skiers can go down

trails (TRAYLZ) the paths along which skiers ski

wicking (WIHK-ing) the process by which wetness is carried away from the skin to the outside of a garment, where it can evaporate

FOR MORE INFORMATION

Books

Brimner, Larry Dane. *Skiing*. New York: Children's Press, 1997.

Crossingham, John. *Skiing in Action*. New York: Crabtree Publishing Company, 2004.

Klingel, Cynthia Fitterer. *Downhill Skiing*. Mankato, MN: Child's World, 2003.

Web Sites

About.com: How to Ski
skiing.about.com/od/beginningskiers/a/howtoski.htm
Basics about learning to ski

eHow: How to Ski Powder
www.ehow.com/how_202_ski-powder.html
Skiing tips plus info about equipment and exercises

Mindconnection: How to Ski, Injury-Free
www.mindconnection.com/library/health/skis.htm
How to avoid injuries while skiing

INDEX

ABOUT THE AUTHOR

Michael Teitelbaum has been a writer and editor of children's books and magazines for more than twenty years. He was editor of *Little League Magazine for Kids;* is the author of a two-volume encyclopedia on the Baseball Hall of Fame, published by Grolier; and was the writer/project editor of *Breaking Barriers: In Sports, In Life,* a character education program based on the life of Jackie Robinson, created for Scholastic Inc. and Major League Baseball. Michael is the author of *Great Moments in Women's Sports,* published by Gareth Stevens, and *Sports in America: The 1980s,* published by Facts on File. His latest work of fiction is *The Scary States of America,* published by Delacorte in 2007. Michael and his wife, Sheleigah, live in New York City, where they root for the Mets.